EDEN *miniatures*

ISTANBUL

Optimist

Istanbul

{Mojito}

breakfast mojito
i had never had
a mojito
before but: why not?
i was on my last twenty pounds of which
i'd just spent fourteen on breakfast, so
a cocktail at noon
seemed
apt...

i got to istanbul on my own after
christoph and i parted ways back in
budapest: he'd had enough and wanted to
go home, i
wanted to see
amsterdam.
how i ended up in istanbul i'm not sure, i

suppose
i must have got on the wrong train –
different train: what can be
wrong
about a train that takes you
where you've not been before

he'd sent over the waiter. that
in itself
was
brazen
i thought. he looked maybe forty, thirty-
eight? forty?
i later find out he was pushing fifty; i
wasn't meaning to flatter him though

i went across to his table, and all the while
he was looking at me the way your uncle
who hasn't seen you in years looks at you,
or a friend of your mum's who remembers
you as a baby: a familiarity that says, you

don't know who i am, but i changed your
nappies when you were little.
maybe that's why i accepted his invitation
to
mojito
in the first place: he felt harmless. forlorn,
perhaps, and a bit quizzical maybe, but
benign

i sat down and he said, 'don't tell me: it's
george.' and that made me wonder.
'isn't it?'
'yes.'
'good to meet you george, my name is
sebastian.'
i'd always liked
sebastian
as a name

he looked at me with his nearly-a-stare
that spoke of

curiosity, even
wonder –
i asked him: 'what are you doing in
istanbul?'
'if only i knew,' he laughed, and there was
a silence.
'how about you?'

soon
the waiter
ahmed
arrived
with mojitos

No Compromise

When I look at pictures of myself of the time when I was as old as I am now that I am sitting opposite me at the Limonlu Bahçe, I don't recognise myself any more or any better than when I listen to my voice on The Tape from the era.

It feels like an era because it is so remote in the past—so distant—that it might as well be an epoch. Thirty years, thereabouts. Just over a generation. I now could easily, comfortably, be my own father then. That messes with my mind a bit, but it literally figures: I left home, aged twenty-one, ten days before my mother's fiftieth birthday.

It never once occurred to me, then, that it would perhaps be a good idea to *stay* for my mother's fiftieth birthday and then leave home, as the last of her children to do so. My mind simply did not entertain that notion. It was not callousness or insensitivity, as such, it was a complete unawareness that that would even be a reasonable thing to do.

I did get my wonderful friend Asta to pick up a thin golden ring that I had bought from the jeweller's, on the inside of which I'd had the words engraved: *In Gratitude.* Asta picked up the ring with some flowers, for which I presumably had given her the money, and took them to my mother on her birthday. That to me seemed reasonable then. My mother still wears the ring, of course. And while I can't to this day explain my behaviour to her, I can see that the memento means something to her, and it means something to me that it does.

Now, as I'm sitting opposite myself at the Limonlu Bahçe in Istanbul with a sense of wonder, I no longer, in that other sense, wonder. This really has changed. For so long I simply wondered, at everything, about all things, all of the time.

I used to wonder what the future might hold, I used to wonder how things were in the present, I used to wonder what I was and what I was to become, I used to wonder, naturally, *why?* Why everything, why anything, really; and I used to wonder how I could come back to this place—any place—and do it for real.

This used to be a pervading feeling of mine: I must come back to this place and do it for real. It was almost like I was on a recce, accumulating intelligence, information on how to do this when it counted, when it was real. It was never real. Now—now ironically being the time and the age and the era when I do a good solid part of my living virtually—it's beginning to be real. And I am immensely relieved. A little scared, perhaps, yes, but in a good way, the way that you get stage fright before you go on in a play, or do a gig.

I thought at first, as first I was beginning to realise who that is, having a mojito with me, that I would want to ask myself innumerable questions. And now I realise, they don't matter now. Now that they could be asked, they evaporate. Could

it be I'm beginning to accept myself
just as I am. *Love* myself, even? Is that
conceivable, still? It's a big word. Love.

I don't think I ever hated myself,
I've hardly ever hated anything or let
alone anyone, but I also don't think
I've ever been able to love myself. I've
overestimated myself, bemused myself,
irritated myself, entertained myself, and
imagined myself somehow exalted, but
loved myself? I don't know what that
would feel like, so I don't think I have.

I want to have a conversation with myself
about something that isn't me, and I ask
young George how he's been spending his
time travelling across Europe. The details
he tells me neither surprise nor remind
me: they sound like the indifferent
anecdotes of a young man who's been

travelling across Europe. The stories he's telling me are intimate, even provocative. In a nonchalant way. I had forgotten that aspect of me: I used to be quite provocative, in a nonchalant way. I used to be rebellious, certainly, and deliberately daring. Never quite as daring as deep down I thought I ought to be though; this too, I seemed to conduct almost as a rehearsal: my daring.

George speaks in a measured, quiet tone, not dissimilar to the tone I hear on The Tape. I'm beginning to wonder whether I have already listened to The Tape, and this is essentially a memory constructed from The Tape, so as not to call it a 'dream,' or whether I'm yet to find The Tape; but then the chronology, in a situation where I'm sitting opposite my thirty years younger self in a delightful

garden cafe in Istanbul, having mojitos
and talking about travels and Europe and
daring and art, does not particularly seem
to matter.

'I cannot bear a compromise, in art,' I hear
myself tell myself; and young me, George,
looks up and smiles that nearly-smile
that I'm beginning to recognise, even
like. 'I find it abhorrent. Compromise is
something, certainly, for politics, perhaps
for a relationship, I don't know; but
for art: no.' I agree with myself on this,
emphatically: 'Yes,' George says, 'I agree
with you. Do you smoke?' And we finally
have our first cigarette together.

The silence is soothing and reassuring,
and I'm reminded of a teacher at school
whose name I can't now remember who
taught us clay modelling. At the school I

went to, this was one of the things we did, and I enjoyed it, in principle, but I was going through a crisis.

We were modelling heads, near life-size (about two thirds or three quarter) and, having finished one of a girl, quite generic, which I thought looked all right but which didn't excite me, I had started a second one, this of an African boy. I couldn't get his features right. I was getting frustrated and I must have expressed this somehow, though I don't remember the how, and our teacher, a German woman in her forties who to me then seemed neither ancient nor young but really curiously both at the same time, and whom I didn't know well enough to like or dislike her, but whom I was able, for her empathy and her concern for my work, to respect, looked at my head and at me and then said: *'Ein Kunstwerk muss durch den Tod gehen.'* A work of art has to go through death.

I intuitively knew what she meant, and although I couldn't entirely comprehend it, I liked the fact that she had used the words 'work of art' and 'death' in one sentence, and combined them so that one was to conquer the other, and I thought nothing of the fact that she seemed to refer to my high school project as a work of art.

She did two or three things to my head that took all of about ninety seconds, and the way was paved for me to finish the project. I completed the head, and it spent the next two or three years in pride of place in my bedroom on a black cloth with a round badge pinned to it on which

the words "BLACK IS BEAUTIFUL"
were printed in small yellow capital
letters on a black background; and when
I moved out of my parents' home, I left
it behind, and since then it has been
living on top of a large commode in the
living room of my parents' holiday flat in
the mountains. I see it there often, and
while I'm not sure it is quite a work of
art, I certainly know it had to go through
a death before it turned into something
that still, after all this time, is in its own
right, quite beautiful.

We finish our cigarettes and I ask George
if he would care to go for a walk, and he
says: 'why not?'

{Amble}

he is walking quietly
slowly
across the bridge which spans over
his restless despair

the river
looks so wet in the rain
and the birds in the water
have brought joyous pursuit they
have clear meaning but they confused it
with sacrifice

he is walking aimlessly
slowly across the sky while his neglect
is fixed on the ground, such a wonderful
heavensent shower this is it is
soaking the mind

it's a worldly world it's a bridge he
walks across it's a water worth in
reality only a smile
slowly he walks

the haze doesn't clear yet
in the distance but as the soothing liquid
is running outside and inside
his hopeful body his temper
has lost its
imagination
what a pity ooh
and his fingers gently touch the railing
if only someone had seen
that at this time he was an Angel.

the light shone through my eyelids
straight into my soul into my central
nervous system
and i asked the lamp post standing next
to me

isn't life full of complexity
the answer i received was fluttered
and overwhelmed, aghast, it burned out
and my palms were suddenly
becoming a pillow
so i rested my baffled nose and cheek and
second rib
while slowly he was
crossing
the bridge

World

'There has to come a point when it stops being about anything, when it just is,' George tells me, as we climb up the steep, picturesque Yeni Çarşı Caddesi towards the main drag that leads from Galatasaray to Taksim Square.

'When it's not about the numbers and not about the acknowledgments and not about the recognition and not about the rewards and not about the money. It's never been nor can it ever be about the money.'

I'm a little impressed with this insight— not that it's not about the money, that's just stating the obvious—but that there has to come a point when it stops being about anything, 'when it just is.' I don't remember having that insight then, but clearly I did. How and when and why did I lose it, ever? What a loss. What rediscovery.

I marvel at the people around us, and, as I always do, I feel a profound love for them all. I wish I could tell them, or, if not tell them, make them sense it, let them know that they are loved, all of them, but I don't know how, and I realise it doesn't matter.

I've left my Eden. I have done so alone. I am in the world. George walks next to me up the hill in silence, and I wonder how far I can take him with me now. Does he still belong here, by my side, or do I have to let him go. His place may be taken by somebody else some day, but I don't know who, and I certainly don't know when, if at all.

Having left my Eden, I realise for the first time that I had an Eden. A garden of peace. Of innocence. Of everything being possible, and nothing yet being done or undone. The Serene Confidence of the Now. I left it and searched for the Thrill of the When, only to be reunited with the Certainty of Always. Is there a Certainty? Is there an Always? The expanse of time is funnelling not to the future but to the present. That's what so reassures me. And so excites me too: has leaving Eden landed me on a planet that is but a springboard to a place where all possible consciousnesses collide?

I want to hold George by the hand to
signal: I can guide you. But I can't guide
him. I know what he's about to embark
on, and I want to tell him that he's going
to be fine. But he's not going to be fine.
He's going to be in pain and in love and
in anguish and in joy and in despair and
in awe and in uncertainty and in these
moments of bliss that seem to make it
worthwhile and in the turmoil and in
the quiet and in the other and in the self.
Does it need to be worthwhile? What
worth, what while?

As we reach the top of the hill and turn
right to immerse ourselves in the current
of the city, I put my arm around George's
shoulder, and we walk on the now even
street, still in silence. He knows who I am,
I am sure. He won't remember when he
is me to have met me, but he'll sense my

presence, and that's enough. He knows that he's not alone.

I want to hug him to my chest, and I feel my arm pull him into me just a little harder to reassure him, but he is too sure of himself now to notice. I like that about George, though it also scares me a little. You are not alone in this world, I want to say to him, but you're choosing a lonely path. They won't get you, most of the time; they won't join you, or walk with you; they will see you wander and think: there goes George.

And that is all right. Because after all, that's the only path you can go that takes you where the universe needs you. If the universe needs you. And if it doesn't, it still is the only path you can go that you recognise as your own. It will lead you here, to me, caring deeply about you, much more than you do; but who knows whence from now: maybe to the person who is us in his eighties, sitting on a bench or in a cafe or in a bar, waiting for us to join him, in thirty years' time...

I stand still in the middle of the bustling throng, and my heart jumps: have I lost him already? That quick? So accidental? Ah no. A sigh of relief: he's just paused to give someone a light. The young man, a little older than he, cups his hand around George's, as George holds his lighter up towards his face, and he looks George in the eyes and gives him a smile. George is oblivious to anything this might mean; he wanly smiles back and, to the young man's flirtatious 'thank you'—not unfriendly but factually—replies: 'you are welcome.' Oh George...

{Memories of the Past}

a surreptitious glance in a doorway: you
had been waiting for me
but how long?
i can't remember, i remember
seeing you at the cinema and us
exchanging glances
(those were the days, mostly, of
glances)
and us not speaking, i was too shy, you
shy too
so i started walking
across the river, there: a cafe, old style;
what
was i doing in there, could it be, really,
that you
waited
outside while i was having coffee inside?

or did i pop in to see if i liked it, but
didn't, or whether you would follow (but
why would you? it was an old style cafe;
and you didn't), so i
popped out again, straight away? that
seems more likely, certainly it seems more
reasonable...

you were in the entrance as i came out
and i saw you again and you me and it
was clear
you'd been waiting for me, there
in the doorway
but we still didn't speak
how was that even possible: it was
obvious
you had been waiting for me, yet
we didn't speak, i not to you, you not to
me
i was incredibly young, you a bit younger,
there by the rhine, in basel, at that time

of glances, mostly, and quietly aching
silences

you were there too maybe two, three years
later
now on the southbank
in london
you looked different, a bit, though not
much
you had those same eyes, longing
uncertain, a
querying glance, that
glance
that i must have had too
it was the era of glances, of not saying
what any of us wanted, ever, of
uncertainty, being afraid
but of what?
of being found out
of revealing too much

too much to the wrong kind of person, of being
vulnerable
literally, viscerally, in danger of injury, death
or afraid merely of actually having,
enjoying, living a moment, such one
brief encounter?
who knows

those were days of unspoken desires
at night time
near rivers
only this time i actually asked you
for a light
or you me?
i you or you me, one of us asked the other
for a cigarette or a light or for both and
another glance was exchanged and a flame
lit up and in that flame we did not look
at each other again, we just looked at the

hands touching, cupping the cigarette,
and that
once again
just was that
how curious
how timid, how cautious, how wary i was
of you
always
and yet how much i wanted to be with
you
still

and then there you were in st james's park:
another you, another glance
i on my way home
you on your way where? i didn't ask and
you didn't say
it was nice
there
to finally meet you
at night, late

by the pond, not the river
to feel your hands on me, taste your lips
such a long time ago now
such a situation between two and
three, thereabouts, in the morning
when that park is not closed and not open
but we both were
closed and open and there: those were the
days
of such stolen moments, so
rare
i miss them no more than i miss you
and i don't miss you, i'm just maybe sorry
a bit
that it took me so long to pluck up the
courage to finally meet you
albeit briefly
we wasted, it seems, a few opportunities,
you and i, but

you live and you learn, and nothing

but nothing
can be rewound, reconfigured, restored, it
can not even be really
relived, it can
of course be
in one way or another
remembered, redeemed?
(to what end? none other than to know
that there was such a thing as a path, a
trajectory,
or an arc:
a semblance of something resembling a
story
a sequence of inconsequential instances,
now implanted, the shapes
along which the currents of time have
mostly been channelled, each curve, each
bend
not just leaving traces but forming them
too
until

at last
there's a torrent
and the river, the brook or the stream
floods its banks and
ignores
these patterns, these half
designs, half
instinctive behaviours half
needed half wanted half detested half
worn and half
overthrown memories
only half
ever
because the half that sits underground
under consciousness under skin under
mind
remains there forever somehow, and
so be it

albeit not always appreciated not always
valued not always wanted or loved

you are always
a part of me still, and
welcome
to stay

whatever became of you, i do wonder
and then i forget that i ever did
because life goes on and
there are many more rivers to cross and
bridges to burn and transgressions that
must be traversed and
comings together
to fathom, just

know that i never not wanted
to know you

Istanbul

We wander on for a bit, and I breathe it
all in: the people, the tourists, the tram
and vendors; the noise and the scent and
the flavour.

George, I'm beginning to realise, is telling
me everything I need to know. He's
hardly said more than a couple of dozen
sentences since we met, improbably and
unfathomably, a few hours ago, but I
know now that seeing him, listening to
him, looking at him, being with him—in
his presence, in no other than that simple,
literal sense—has triggered in me the
abundance of memories, connexions and
emotions, the thoughts and the synaptic
excursions, the diversions, the captions,

the mild insurrections of heart, mind and
soul, that I need, to move on.

Move on from what? Had I got stuck?
Most severely. Had I manoeuvred myself
into a dead end? More than of sorts. Was
I on the verge of becoming obsolete, not
just to myself, but to the universe that has
somehow produced me? I fear me I was.
Is that now all at an end? Who knows…

I again put my arm around George,
instinctively, without thinking, and he
doesn't shirk or pause or look at me, he
just lets it be. My George: that's how I
know him. We wander, like father and
son, like brothers, like friends, but not
lovers—can one constellation embody
all these in one, even, ever?—and I
feel me an abundant sensation of love.
Of loss too, and of forgiveness. Most

of all of forgiveness: I forgive you, George, for everything, really. All your inadequacies. Your presumptions, your misunderstandings. Your aloofnesses and your hesitancies. Your delusions and your noble intentions. Your foibles, all of your weaknesses. Your constant quest to connect, your patent inability to do so in so many senses. There are too many things to mention.

Too many things too, for which I do not need to forgive you, for which I can quietly, humbly, respect you: even admire you. Your sense of justice and your faith in humans. Your optimism, your hope. Your openness, your curiosity. It may, ultimately, have killed the cat, but the cat had nine lives and so it continued. It lived. You're not unlike a cat, George, I've known this for centuries, for all the millennia that I've known you. And I'm beginning to know you now, George, and I'm glad on't.

We reach Taksim Square where we take a turn to the right and keep wandering. Not aimlessly so much as non-directionally. We both have no particular place to go, not at the moment. We end up by a steep small street that looks a little familiar and quite attractive, and decide to head up it, rather than down, and before long we recognise a wooden house and a half hidden entrance: we have inadvertently come back to right where we started: the Limonlu Bahçe.

There is, probably, in some way some significance to this: have we actually gone round in a circle? I like to think not, not least because we are not moving in three dimensions. We have, at any rate, walked a spiral, a triangular shaped one, as it turns out, but that is most likely quite by the by. Some things have meaning, others less so. Some things are profound though we but capture the surface, others are really surface. Or maybe I'm being lazy. At some level, most likely, everything has some other layer, some other meaning, some other significance that could or could not be, or become, at some point quite relevant. We can't take it all in, all at the same time: we do need a filter. And that's yet another insight I'm having, right there.

We've not walked very far, maybe less than an hour, perhaps a bit more; we've been ambling really, rather than striding. We've not been saying all that much more. Metaphorically, though, we have come a long way. In my mind I have travelled a little light year. Is there a big light year? Or even one of average length? Aren't all light years the same? It is not, of course, and I realise, a year, and it's not one of light. Some metaphors don't stack up. I have percolated, I feel me, through my own conscience and come out enriched. If that makes sense. Does it have to? Make sense? To me, it doesn't have to, even though somehow it does. I don't think it matters to George if it does. Does it matter to you?

I realise I have a reader. I realise I need you as my reader, because without you I don't exist. I realise I am not alone in this, nor only with George: I realise we are, in our own constellation, triangular. Hello, Reader: welcome to my world.

George and I are both creatures of habit, and having walked for an hour or so— maybe a little less, possibly just a bit more—we both fancy another drink, and we readily, easily, without thinking or negotiation, decide to go back to the Limonlu Bahçe: we liked it there, we were comfortable there, why would we not now go back there, seeing we are already here.

I like that about George and about me: we can stay in one place for hours and never get bored. We both never get bored, George and I. That is a realisation I had and passed on to him long before I knew I would be him: if you watch paint dry close enough, it's entirely riveting. At molecular level, let alone subatomic: there's a riot of things happening, a mesmerising display of spectacular wonder. How could you ever get bored?

We head down the hidden staircase back into the garden which is now not full and not empty, but at that agreeable mid-to-late afternoon state when luncheon has petered out and dinner hasn't yet started. The table we had been sitting at has been taken, but we find one as pleasant in the mid-to-late afternoon speckled shade two or three tables removed and sit down, and our angular waitress returns and recognises us and smiles, and we order another couple of mojitos and some chips, just to nibble.

Now, for the first time in maybe a million years, I am here. George, because of the configuration of the table, the bench and the chairs, has naturally sat down next to me, not opposite, so he can survey the garden with me, this paradise of our own making. This Eden. *"Look at me now, and here I am,"* she had said, and I had understood her, immediately. Joyce, Shakespeare, Stein. Then Shakespeare again, then no particular order.

I can be at home with myself in a paradise of my making that doesn't know what it is, in a city I've never been before, within an instant and find me not tempted by knowledge, in no need of a companion, at ease. Not forever, of course, just for now. The curiosity and the fascination, the alertness and also the need will soon get the better of me, that I know, it has ever been thus.

But now. And here. We are.

www.ingramcontent.com/pod-product-compliance
Lightning Source LLC
Chambersburg PA
CBHW021130070726
47591CB00014B/2199